Barbed Wire and Gunny Sacks

Barbed Wire and Gunny Sacks

A MEMOIR OF THE
FARMER'S DAUGHTER

⟶⟞

Dorothy Peth Dalan

ISBN: 1530854466
ISBN 13: 9781530854462

For My Grandchildren

Jay and Arielle
Sara, Emma and Nate

Few words are written about the lives of ordinary people.
My birth, marriage and death will be recorded but I give you
These memoirs so you will know who I was.

Acknowledgements

You may read my memoirs and think "That's not the way it happened.", but this is how I remember it. My stories are mostly true, with some embellishment and some names have been changed to avoid embarrassment.

I am deeply indebted to Claire Swedberg, my editor, instructor, friend and inspiration. She taught me everything about writing; everything I had forgotten from English 101. The encouragement I received weekly from the writing group at the La Conner Senior Center has been invaluable. Thank you Roberta, Lydia, Susan, Doris, Jerry, Patsy, Ann, Ric, Janna and Barbara.

The photos in the book are from the Earl and Kathy Peth collection, with appreciation to Bob Peth for making them available. I also thank my brother Earl Peth for refreshing my memory about the early days.

A nod to my granddaughter, Sara for the necessary technical support. She is a great teacher.

To my husband, Roger, who has always indulged my whims and fantasies, the most patient husband ever, I thank you for constant love and support.

Table of Contents

My Roots

DURING A BLINDING SNOWSTORM WHICH dumped 14 inches on Skagit County, my father, George Earl Peth came screaming into this world. He was the second of four sons born to John and Mary Jane Peth, early Washington territory pioneers.

The family lived in the imposing Victorian mansion at the corner of LaConner/Whitney and McLean Rds. where their father put them to work on the farm as soon as they could fit their hands around a hammer or a pitchfork. Although he was at one time the largest land owner in the county and topped the list of most taxes paid in a single year, he never paid his sons for the work they did on the farm. They worked right along with the hired hands and expected no special treatment. Rainy days certainly never meant a day off but they could be found sitting in the barn pulling nails out of old boards and straightening them for future use. He was frugal and a recycler way ahead of his time.

To earn spending money the boys had to go to work for neighboring farmers after their labor at home was done, When Archie, the third son, found the love of his life, he had to sell his prized saddle to get money for the marriage license. They all learned at the school of hard knocks and learned well the value of a dollar and the satisfaction which comes from hard work.

Their escape from the farm came on a swift horse at the end of the day for John Peth was a horse trader of some renown. Historical records report, "If you needed a horse, for riding or to pull a plow, you went to John Peth in LaConner."

The horsemanship skills learned at an early age were a natural segue into the world of roughneck rodeo business where they all became bareback bronc riders, often winning the jackpot to supplement their income.

A half mile north of the Peth homestead, on LaConner/Whitney Road, lived the Sievert Handstad family. There a poor Norwegian- born farmer was struggling to raise 10 children after his wife had been taken from them when the Spanish flu epidemic swept through Skagit county in 1918. Nadine Handstad was six years old at the time and saw her childhood fly away as she and her older sister, Florence, became the ladies of the house and learned to do the cooking, cleaning and all necessary chores.

While playing under the big oak tree in the front yard one day, Nadine felt the ground beneath her feet begin to tremble and heard the unmistakable thunder of horse hooves pounding on the dry dirt road and recognized the four Peth boys approaching in a cloud of dust.

They rode four abreast down the middle of the road as if they owned it, cowboy hats pulled low upon their heads, shiny spurs clanking against their boots, fringed leather chaps slapping against the sides of their wild, high spirited horses.

Quickly Nadine darted behind the wide trunk of the tree, hoping these ruffian riders would not see her. When she realized they were stopping to talk to her older brothers in the yard she hesitated only a second before climbing the tree; the branches and bark tearing at her hands and knees. Once established in a secure spot, she remained until they were gone and felt it was safe to come down. This happened many times over her growing up years and no one could convince her that the Peth boys were harmless.

As the girls grew up and Florence became of marrying age, which was considered to be in the early teens, she fell in love with the eldest Peth boy, John Junior and married him. They set to farming a large ranch between Bow Hill and Samish Island and many of their siblings came to work for them. Nadine went to live with them and help raise the children which soon came along.

While she was there, one of the frequent visitors was John's brother George. The brothers had always been close friends and now that friendship included Florence and Nadine. They taught the girls to ride, went on hunting trips where they camped in the woods and the girls cooked while the guys hunted. It was a whole new world for Nadine and she liked it.

When she turned 17, George proposed and she readily accepted. One month later they were married in a civil ceremony in Bellingham and spent 50 years happily married on their farm on Best Road where they raised cattle, peas, potatoes, three daughters and one son.

I am their third daughter, Dorothy, born in 1935.

This is my story.

The House at Peth's Corner

$\sim\!\!6$

MY GRANDFATHER JOHN JACOB PETH, an early pioneer, started for the far west in 1877, leaving his parents' home in Calumet, Wisconsin to build a life on his own. He was 19 and had graduated from a local college as an engineer. He traveled by train to the end of the line, which was Portland at that time. For an old shotgun and a jug of whiskey, he hired an Indian to take him up Puget Sound by canoe to Mt. Vernon.

The first job he found was in a logging camp but he quickly tired of that hard work and decided to try farming. He homesteaded some government land near Mt. Vernon, became quite successful and accumulated over 3,000 acres of land of which 1000 were timber land so many of his early years were devoted to logging.

By 1899 he had accumulated enough wealth to take a bride and build a home. He met my Grandmother Mary Jane Black, at a logging camp in Wickersham, Whatcom County where she was working as a cook. She was 26 and he was 46 when they married and built their home at what came to be known as Peths Corner, where LaConner/Whitney Road meets McLean Road.

They built a three story Victorian home, complete with turrets and balconies and a wide front porch which stood on a foundation of stones gathered from the quarry at the Hole in the Wall in LaConner.

As you entered the house through the side door you found yourself in a lengthy, wide dining room where there stood a table so long it nearly filled the room and a lowboy buffet to one side. At the end of the room you could enter the office which later became the only bedroom on the first floor.

The kitchen was spacious and contained a round wooden table circled by several tall back chairs and a massive desk with papers strewn all about. The working part of the kitchen was behind a partial wall which housed a wide open fireplace with stone up to the ceiling. In one corner of the kitchen, behind a curved rustic door, was the small winding stairway up to the sleeping quarters for the hired help.

At the front of the house, in a hallway off the parlor was the broad winding staircase with its polished wooden banister that cried out to be slid down, which led to the second floor and all the bedrooms. Between the floors, on the landing was a grand organ which got a thorough workout from any child who passed. The 3rd floor was taken up by a dormitory style bedroom where the four boys, one being my dad, slept.

It was a house like none I had ever seen and even as a small child I appreciated its grandeur.

My earliest memory of my paternal grandparents and their home was when I was about three or four and my dad dropped me off at the house one morning and went on to the barn, leaving me alone with my grandmother in that awesome house and how uncomfortable I felt. She was not someone I knew well and I was a shy child, usually hiding behind my mother or my older sisters.

"Dorothy, would you like some breakfast?" Grandmother asked. "Yes," I said and climbed up on a chair around the table in the middle of the room. She disappeared behind the wall of stone where the stove was located and the sound of pots and pans told me she was cooking something. Soon she poked her head around the wall and asked me how I wanted my eggs cooked. What a question to ask a child! No one ever asked me that before. At home my egg was always placed before me on a plate and I ate it. I had no idea how it was cooked. I didn't know what to say. "Any way is okay" I replied but when she brought it to me, I knew that was the wrong answer for there it was staring at me from the plate, its big yellow eye wobbling from side to side. This was not what I was used to but somehow I knew I had to eat it, and eat it I did.

For some reason, we didn't visit there often but I remember my mother stopping at the house a few times with the four of us in tow and we were told to sit quietly in the parlor and take turns looking at the stereoscope which entertained us for hours.

By the time I was ten my grandparents were both in failing health so we had Christmas dinner at their house, bringing the turkey and all the trimmings, all adults and kids, 16 cousins in all, sitting around that long dining room table while both grandparents were sick in bed. Perhaps it was a comfort to them just to know we were all there.

In May that year we celebrated Grandfather's 92nd birthday in the Rowley hospital in Mt. Vernon, shortly before he died. Grandmother was then moved to a cottage next to the Burlington hospital and cared for by a distant relative. Several times she was found on the highway trying to get back to her house at Peth's Corner, only to be captured and returned to the safety of her new little home until only a few months later she too died.

The old Victorian stood empty there on the corner for many years. Riding past it on the school bus, I loved looking at it, sometimes imagining I saw someone move in the window. Once I even made the driver let me off there to pick the daffodils in the yard. None of the four sons or daughter wanted to live there so the decision was made to tear it down in the 1950s.

Then one day a pickle factory claimed Peth's Corner and now a family potato farm works there, but many of us who grew up here in the valley remember when the beautiful Victorian crowned that corner.

My Earliest Memory

I BELIEVE MY EARLIEST MEMORY was of a freak accident which occurred when I was about three years old.

I have a vividly colored picture in the recess of my mind of my early home. It was the house on Best Road which set on a 320 acre farm which my parents were given upon their marriage in 1931. Of course my Grandfather Peth also gave them the mortgage to go along with the farm.

It was a plain little frame house; one story with an attic destined to become two bedrooms as the family grew. The kitchen was the largest room in the house and was where we all spent most of our time. Maybe it was because the huge, black and chrome Monarch wood stove made it the warmest room in the house. On cold wintry mornings we dressed by the stove and in the spring we often had a box behind the stove with one or two curly little lambs incubating there.

In the center of the room stood a bulky circular wooden table where the family ate all meals, played board games, did our homework and huddled around the radio in the evening listening to such thrillers as, "I Love a Mystery "or "The Shadow."

Also in the kitchen, on the wall next to the back door stood a desk: the business center of the house. It had a counter- top writing area and three deep drawers beneath. The top drawer was always jam-packed with bills, letters and other important papers. The second drawer was equally uninteresting. But, the third heavy drawer was full of enticing things like scissors, crayons, coloring books and puzzles.

On this particular day, I had apparently gotten something out of this drawer and was trying to close it, pushing so hard, with my face close to the drawer, my tongue forced out between my teeth when suddenly it slid shut with a bang on my tongue.

I recall sitting on my Mother's lap in the car as my Dad drove us quickly to the doctor's office in LaConner. My mother had to hold my hands down to keep me from pulling off the little dangling tip of tongue. There was a lot of blood and a lot of crying. Old Dr. Brooks took a couple of stitches and put me together good as new.

Chores of Yesterday

GROWING UP ON A FARM, I had chores. They were simple and well defined. At the time I thought I was severely put upon. I was the little slave girl. I was pretty sure none of my friends had such a hard life. My main chore, which had to be done every single day, come hell or high water, was filling the large wood box which stood on the back porch like a behemoth, a 500 pound gorilla, which grew larger with every passing day.

Wood box protocol was spelled out in bold letters, simple enough for a child to understand. Upon arriving home from school around 4 o'clock, you changed from school clothes into play clothes, something with long sleeves if you had any sense at all, and then headed for the wood-shed.

That made two reasons you dreaded going to the wood-shed.

It was located about 100 feet behind the house but always seemed far away, especially if it was dark. It was a suspicious and spooky place where a skunk, weasel or porcupine might be lurking, just waiting to attack. The firewood was thrown helter-skelter from the sawdust floor to the rafters and in the center was the stump or chopping block wherein was lodged the killer axe, which my dad used to chop the wood into pieces just the right size to fit the wood box and the cook stove.

My mother and the enormous fire belching Monarch range, which took up most of one end of the kitchen, depended on a full wood box for cooking our meals and heating part of the small house even though we did also have an oil burner in the living room. Even a child should have been able to understand the need for firewood but it always seemed to be a huge imposition on my playtime.

Having two older sisters provided a large wood packing crew and per-haps if we had worked together as, say a team, we could have made the job go more quickly. If one person held out both arms, cupped upward while the other person loaded them up, perhaps it would have been a good strat-egy but that would have required cooperation. Not our thing!

We spent a lot of time throwing wood at each other, complaining about slivers, the cold or the heat as the case might be, the skill of the wood chop-per, the size and quality of the wood, who wasn't doing his share of the packing and the audacity of my dad for assigning us this job.

Sometimes the fighting and bickering led to threats involving the axe but, fortunately, it took quite a bit of muscle to actually free it from the chopping block.

Sixty- some years later, I am still responsible for providing necessary heat for our home but the chore is a million times easier and there are no slivers involved. All I do is write the check, mail it in to Farmers Supply and wait for the propane truck to come. Ah…life is so much simpler today.

When the war ended and building supplies again became available, my parents hired Alfred Nelson of LaConner to build us a new home there on the farm to better accommodate our growing family. It was a brick house with plenty of space for us all but a lot of work for my mother. We were now age 11, 12 and 13 and our chores also grew.

One daily chore was the dishes, a job everyone hated. We were all well trained in this three man job but of course no man ever took a turn. Woman's work! One person washed, one dried and the third person put the clean dishes away in the cupboard. Positions were rotated each week and the only way you could get out of it it was by broken arms or legs, severe illness or death.

Each meal involved dishes for seven people, sometimes more, at least three courses and enough pots and pans to cook this banquet. Of course it was only the evening meal when we were on duty. During the day my mother, "Mrs. Clean" kept the kitchen spotless; not one pan soaking in the sink, not one grease spot on the stove top and she expected it to look that way at the end of our shift.

My mother worked hard and I figured it was not too much of an imposition for us to help out in the evening but the thing that was hardest for me to understand was that she expected us to be cheerful about it. I think her goal in life was that some magical day at least one of us would jump up from the table with a smile on her face and without being told would attack the dish washing chore. I'd like to say it was me who made her dream come true but it probably wasn't. More than likely it was Janet.

I remember a once-in-a-lifetime chore which was assigned to the three of us one hot summer day by my dad. I was probably nine or ten. "Cut the mustard." he told us and he sent us out to the 40 acre field behind the barn, wearing overalls, straw hats and armed with a hoe. We all recognized that big yellow weed and all we had to do was give it a good whack with the hoe and watch it fall over dead. It went pretty well for about half an hour but then we got hot, tired, thirsty, resentful and bored.

That was when we decided to liven up the day and practice swearing. No one could hear us way out here in the field. No one would be coming at us with that big bar of soap we all dreaded. We knew all the words having overheard the hired men and even our dad use them out in the barn. The forbidden words!

We made up complete sentences using them in the right way. We swore at each other, the damn mustard, the blazing sun and the hell of a hot day.

We had so much fun trying out our new vocabulary we kind of forgot about cutting the mustard. I believe there had even been some talk of money if we did a good job but I don't recall becoming wealthy or ever doing it again. My dad must have chalked it up to another bad farming experiment.

Mud Pies

ONE OF MY FAVORITE CHILDHOOD pastimes was making mud pies. Living on a Northwest Washington farm there was no shortage of mud and I had a wide selection of pans with which to create my masterpieces. My sisters and friends made pathetic looking mud pies, flat and uninteresting, but I remember mine were splendiferous works of art.

After completing the mud pie, I would search the barnyard for any embellishment I could find. Tiny pebbles looked like chopped nuts on top of my cupcakes; layer cakes were sprinkled with tobacco weed or decorated with tiny leaves and flowers. Oats made the perfect topping for an almond torte.

My inclination toward producing artistically enticing food grew along with me and soon I was poring over my mother's cookbooks and the Better Homes and Gardens magazine as soon as it arrived each month, devouring the colored pictures of attractive food. I always thought whoever came up with the theory, "Less is More" was either just plain lazy or had no imagination.

Very early on I developed a style based on three cardinal rules:

1. Garnish is good
2. You can never have too much embellishment
3. Presentation is everything

I applied these three cardinal rules to my style of dress as well as my gastronomic creations. I decorated myself with bright colors, ruffles, flowing chiffon scarves and clunky costume jewelry. Any item of clothing with beads, glitter or sequins called my name. You could call me "Fancy Nancy," "Ornate Nellie" or "Gaudy Gertie" but never "Plain Jane."

Each year on our birthdays my mother would ask, "What kind of cake do you want?" and my sisters would yell, "chocolate" or "I want white," but I would search the cookbooks until I found the perfect one. For several years mine was "Lady Baltimore!" It was a layer cake, but not an ordinary round one; it was baked in a 9-inch square pan. It contained chopped dates, nuts and candied cherries with seven-minute frosting which was tinted a delicate pink with the cherry juice. A small bouquet of real flowers decorated the top. My mother complied with that year after year. It was almost too beautiful to cut.

In high school, Home Economics became my favorite subject as I learned to sew, make pudding and white sauce as smooth as cream. It was then I decided I would become a Home Ec teacher. There was a world of people out there who needed to learn the art of swirling, dipping, glazing, topping and sprinkling; I was just the one who could show them.

I was knee-deep in disillusion when I got to college and found the lessons were more basic and concerned with food methodology and nutrition. Where was the garnish? I did have one instructor who shared my interest in embellishment and taught me a few new techniques. Such as how to decorate the fruit cakes we baked each year at Christmas and sold to faculty members. Placing candied cherries and almonds artfully on the top and brushing with glaze made them more alluring. They sold like hotcakes.

Once graduated and married, I overheard a conversation between my husband and his friend, who said, "Boy, you are really lucky, Roger, being married to a Home Ec teacher. I bet she is a great cook!" Roger replied,

"Oh, she's okay, but boy can she garnish!"

But my greatest compliment came one day in the café at the college where I worked. I was having lunch with friends and as I started through the salad bar, my friend Rick who was the Art Gallery curator and an artist himself, squeezed in behind me with his tray and said, "I'm going to follow you and do everything you do because I've noticed your salad is always a work of art!"

Amazing! From mud pies to salad bars!

Behind the Wheel

It was the best of times, it was the worst of times. The year was 1945 and I was a 10 year old farm kid. Most farm kids are experienced drivers by the age of 12 but because I had two older, aggressive sisters, I had yet to have my time behind the wheel.

This particular day was one of those warm, summer days when the sun just seems to hang up there in the sky, reluctant to end each glorious moment. In the evening my dad would feed the cattle in a field away from our home place and needed help which usually involved one of my older sisters driving the truck while he pitched the hay off the back of the truck with a pitchfork but on this particular evening neither of them wanted to go with him.

Suddenly it was my turn. I had lived for this day!

Once in the field, my dad showed me how to put the gear stick into 1st position and let the clutch out slowly. Slowly was the key word here so there would be no sudden jerk which could possibly throw him off the truck. My mother was sitting in the passenger seat with my little brother Earl, between us.

As we rode around the field at about five miles per hour, all I had to do was keep a steady eye forward and steer. With my small, sweating hands tightly gripping the wheel I circled the field at a slow steady speed. I was bursting with pride. I was driving! It was the best of times!

When the job was done, the cattle had been fed, my dad got behind the wheel and drove us home where we were surprised to find a note telling us that my sisters had gone to town with the neighbors and would return soon. I could hardly wait until they came home so I could tell them about my driving experience but when they arrived there was an entirely different story to tell.

That warm summer evening was August 14, 1945 and World War II had just ended!

My sisters (like almost everyone else in Skagit County) had gone into Mt. Vernon with the Hedlund family to celebrate. They told us about the dancing in the street, the bands playing, the balloons and confetti which filled the air and all the excitement they had been a part of.

They couldn't stop talking about how much fun they had had while we were out in the field unaware of the news. My driving didn't seem so thrilling anymore, I felt left out and cheated.

It was the worst of times.

Cluck Cluck Just My Luck

ONE OF MY FAVORITE PLAYMATES was my cousin Patty who lived on McLean Road, about five miles from our farm. We were the same age and spent a lot of time together, usually at her house. She was an only child and my Aunt Eva liked me to come and play.

One day, however, she had come to my house and I loved that because I could teach her all about the farm and show her all the things I knew about animal husbandry. Patty did not live on a farm so she was always eager to learn. The thought of teaching her, her open mind like a sponge, made me giddy and I decided to show her the magic thing I knew about chickens.

I took her into the chicken pen out by the barn, and closed the gate behind us. Tall wire fence surrounded the pen so the chickens could not escape. Patty helped me shoo all of the hens out of the adjoining hen house into the yard. Then I told her about the magical phenomenon which I had learned while watching my dad kill chickens.

My mother made the best fried chicken in the whole world and was known far and wide for her culinary excellence. On most Saturday afternoons my dad would set up production in the front yard while we all anticipated the delicious chicken dinner we would be having on Sunday.

He had a big stump which he used for a chopping block, a large sharply honed axe and big tubs of boiling water standing by which he would use to remove the feathers. Many times I watched my dad grab a chicken out of a gunny sack, holding it by the legs and lay it on the chopping block. Whack! The axe hit the chicken on its neck and blood came spurting out. Then he would swing the chicken around in a wide circle over his head and the chicken's head would come flying off.

I found it absolutely hilarious to see the chicken there in his hands and its head lying in the green grass ten feet away. For an encore the headless chicken would run around in circles until it flopped over dead. What an act!

This was the magic trick I was planning to show Patty. She would be astonished! I told Patty to watch me as I crouched low to the ground, about chicken height, with my arms spread out at my sides and dipped and swirled around the chicken pen. By swooshing the chickens into the corner of the fence, it was often possible to snatch one by the legs. After trying repeatedly and also being very careful to avoid the rooster, we each had a chicken by its long, spindly legs. Excitedly, I yelled, "Swing it around till its head comes off". When nothing happened, I said, "Try another chicken." This would be embarrassing if it didn't work. Where was the magic?

I kept shouting, "Swing it around till its head comes off. "Chickens were staggering around, screeching and squawking and flying at the fence in an attempt to escape. Patty had joined in the chant, "Swing it around till its head comes off", as we danced around the chicken pen. This was such an exciting time. Never did it enter my mind that I had forgotten one technicality, the axe.

Suddenly, without warning, there was my dad at the gate looking to see what all the commotion was about. All the fun came to an abrupt end and

I was so embarrassed as I was snatched out of the chicken pen and given a swat on my behind along with a serious lecture about raising chickens and something about egg production and other facts I wasn't interested in.

Oh well, there were many other things I could teach Patty. Maybe she'd like to see the baby geese.

Grandpa's Mules

(As told by my dad, George Peth)

GRANDPA PETH WAS A HORSE trader. It was said in the late 1800's and early 1900's, if you came to Washington Territory intending to farm, you went to John Peth for a horse. You either bought a single draft horse or if you had a little more money, a good team of horses. My dad had some pasture land that wasn't planted in hay or oats so he could run (pert near) 50 horses there on the home place.

He had some pretty nice horses and some that was just plain knot heads, but if they looked good, he could always find some damn fool to buy them. Your Grandpa was a (purty) shrewd business man but he met his match the day the shyster salesman came by selling Jack donkeys. He said he would sell him a Jack Donkey and then buy back all the draft mules he could produce from his good work mares.

It sounded like a good deal, how could he lose? But then, more than once he had been bamboozled by some fast talking salesman and had enough worthless mining stock to paper the walls in the parlor to prove it.

So the Jack moved in and Grandpa soon had a field full of draft mules. He could have sold one to everyone in the county and still had leftovers.

But of course he couldn't find hide nor hair of the mule buyer. That's when my dad came up with the plan to make me and John mule salesmen.

I had just turned 16 that winter and John was 17. I was a sophomore and John was a junior that year. Well, he pulled us both out of school and we drove them damn mules down to Whitney Station and loaded them on the Great Northern. Altogether we had three full cars, two for John and one for me. What a sight it was. Can you imagine all the brayin' and kickin' going on in those cars!

John headed east, over the mountains and down to Utah where he sold all his mules to the Mormon farmers. He turned over the mules with a promise that they would pay after they tried them. That was a big mistake because they never did pay him and he was forced to take a job herding sheep on some big ranch out there till he could earn enough money to get train fare home. My dad was not happy about that!

I still laugh when I think about John herding sheep in Utah.

I was sent south to California with my mules and had good luck selling them to a big ranch right around where Los Angeles is today. They were going to use them for working the fields up to plant wheat but, you know how stubborn a mule is, and they insisted I stay and help them break 'em and get them used to the plow and all before they'd pay me. So they gave me a bed in the bunk house and I stayed on for a couple of months.

When they finally paid me and let me go, I found my way to the harbor and caught a steamer home. It took quite a while; I didn't think I'd ever see LaConner again. School was out by the time I got home and they said I had only attended 9 days so I had to take the whole year over again but that's okay, I had quite an adventure.

MY DAD GEORGE PETH

Little Goose Girl

~6

Maybe because I have a non-confrontational personality, I have avoided conflict with others most of my life. However, I do recall one instance in my childhood where I encountered great conflict with my dad and his geese.

I don't know why we had geese on the farm. We didn't eat the eggs they laid or use the down for quilts or pillows.

Sometimes farmers use geese to weed their strawberries but we didn't have any berries. All they did was wander around the barnyard leaving goose grease all over the ground; slimy, stinky stuff. And it seemed we were forever stepping in it.

My dad was a practical man, always concerned with the bottom-line. "If it didn't produce get rid of it" seemed to be his motto. Farming was hard work and he loved it but he was definitely in it for the profit. He did however, make a few exceptions and we had a Shetland pony and a saddle horse. They gave us some pleasure so maybe that justified them being there. But, WHY THE GEESE?

I could see no reason for them to be there unless they were there for me to chase and I did that frequently. As I recall, before school years I spent many days alone, running around the gravel barnyard. It must have been when I was about four years old and my two older sisters were in school. My dad had warned me many times to stop chasing the geese but I chose not to listen. I'm sure the geese didn't like it because I remember one time a big old goose turned on me, hissing loudly. She flew at me, grabbed the hem of my coat in her beak and shook me all over the barnyard. I tried frantically to free myself but that goose with her powerful beak, would not release me. I screamed, "Help! Someone get this goose off of me!" I was crying and screaming as she whipped me around with gravel flying in all directions.

I was rescued but given strict orders, once again to stop chasing the geese. I'm not sure but I probably got a good swat on my butt, too. I HATED THOSE GEESE!

But then something happened. Spring came to the farm. The slough was high on the banks with sparkling water running swiftly, the grass had turned a brilliant, emerald green and there were little golden buttercups everywhere. It was glorious! And a miracle had occurred- there were darling, little, yellow fuzzy, baby geese. They were so tiny and cute waddling along behind their mother. I knew I just had to pick them up and snuggle them.

It wasn't long before I began to run after the geese, trying to pick up the little goslings. This had to be done quickly so as not to be seen by the mother goose. In my haste, with apparent clumsiness, I stepped on a few little babies and killed them.

Large wings started flapping like thunder, there was a hissing like a locomotive on a rampage and I started running. There was such pandemonium in the barnyard that my dad and several hired men were suddenly upon the scene.

Farmers had a method of teaching their hunting dogs not to kill the chickens on the farm although they were instinctively predatory. If they killed a chicken it was tied around the dog's neck until it started to rot and omit a pungent odor so offensive the dog never wanted to repeat the act.

My dad picked up the dead little goslings and in that moment must have thought of the perfect punishment for me. He went to the barn, got some twine and tied it around the tiny leg of one gosling. Then he made a big loop forming a sort of necklace with the little animal hanging down by one leg. He grabbed me and hung it around my neck. He said, "Now! Wear this little goose necklace all day to remind you of what you have done!"

I remember crying a lot that day as I walked around with my necklace, feeling such humiliation and anger at my dad. The hired men thought it was all very funny and called me "the little goose girl" for months, adding to my humiliation.

I think back on this event and recognize that act as abusive punishment by today's standards. My dad was raised by the same tough measures and it was what he knew. He still believed it was effective learning. He would have laughed to see his great grandchildren punished by a "time-out." A trip to the wood-shed and a swat with a piece of kindling was our timeout.

It was effective and I'm still alive to tell about it.

Bologna to Go

One of the most important parts of a child's school day is lunch. It's a break from all that learning, reading, math and geography, and a precious few minutes to rest and reconnect with home and mother through peanut butter or bologna.

As fascinated as I am with metal lunch pails in antique shops today, I cannot remember what my lunch pail looked like as a child but I am sure I had one for I can easily recall the odor of sour milk in that pail on the long bus ride home in the afternoon where I would open it hoping to find a snack I had not eaten at lunchtime.

Every September, along with new school clothes and shoes, we each got a new lunch bucket and usually by October the Thermos in that lunch bucket would be broken. A broken Thermos meant I would have to buy milk at school, so each day I would leave home with a nickel (the price of one half pint of warm, homogenized milk) tied up in a pretty little floral handkerchief and placed in my pocket for safe keeping until the teacher collected milk money.

Being raised on a farm I was used to drinking raw milk, kept cold in the refrigerator and could never adjust to the taste of pasteurized, warm milk. Most days I spent a lot of time at the lunch table trying to figure out a clever way to dispose of that carton of milk without being seen

Children in Europe were starving in these post-war times and it was considered a crime, punishable by death, to be wasteful.   Many years later I became friends with Gerda, one of those German children who said she hated Roosevelt and his Marshall plan for sending them milk, for she really preferred beer.

I chastise myself now for not being smart enough to have skipped the milk, saved the nickel, invested wisely and accumulated great wealth. Maybe enough to buy a refrigerator for the school so they could keep the milk cold.

I can still see my mother in the pantry making our lunches assembly line style, creating bologna sandwiches, the meat of choice. We each got two slices of white Wonder bread, slathered with butter and mayonnaise, no mustard, no lettuce, which would turn to snot by noon, one slice of bologna then cut in half, straight across, no fancy diagonals, and wrapped in wax paper with the drugstore fold. They were always wrapped so expertly, ensuring freshness, I thought my mother must have been a factory packaging worker in another life.

On good days there would usually be a couple of homemade cookies under the sandwich and maybe an apple or an orange. On a really good day there would be a Hershey bar. If by some chance we ran out of bologna, peanut butter out of the big Skippy jar always on the pantry shelf, and homemade berry jam would be the replacement.

Monotony ruled but it never bothered me. It was always better than the lunch my friend Sharon brought every single day; a thermos of tomato soup! Her mother had no imagination at all.

The 6th year of grade school, when we moved over to the high school building, the PTA National Hot Lunch program began and some bureaucrats though we all should partake, assuring we would get one healthy meal per day. What it meant for me was a drastic change, eating foods I had never seen before. We had never had chili at home, nor spaghetti or other dishes with tomato sauce poured all over them. It was a learning experience and I found I liked some things, hated others. I loved the smell coming from the kitchen on days when they baked corn bread or tuna casserole, hated Wednesdays and the smell of chili.

Many days, even through high school, I still carried my faithful bologna sandwich and the touch of home, packed securely in a paper bag.

Second Grade

THERE WE ARE, THE 2ND and 3rd grade class on the steps of the LaConner Grade school, looking east toward the playground. The year is 1942.

Our teacher, Mrs. Ralph Nelson lovingly looks over her 34 children, all dressed up for "picture day." The two oldest and tallest boys in the group, Arnold Billy and Gus Stone are to her right.

The top row is all made up of 3rd graders. The two black children are Ben and Betty Franks of the only black family in La Conner for the next 20 years. If the picture was in color you could easily spot my cousin Billy Hanstad with his bright red hair, toward the end of that row.

Ivan leads the next row, looking quite sinister with his head down and his neatly combed hair, apparently not happy to be having his picture taken. He stands next to Rueben who was with us for only a short time and remembered as being different, perhaps from another country. There is Myrna with a smile on her little round face; happy that day and never knowing she wouldn't make it to graduation. Polio claimed her life without warning in her senior year.

There is Sybil with her long blonde braids, standing tall and looking serious. We all remember the day of 8th grade graduation when she showed up without those braids; a big change in her life. Next to Sybil is Margaret Sampson who I will always remember as the girl who beat me at the radio broadcast of the County Spelling Bee. I tried to be happy for her, but it was very hard; I wanted so badly to win.

Then there is Sharon with her reddish brown pigtails who was my best friend in those early years until her parents sent her to Seattle to the Holy Names Academy. We met for coffee years later and she told me those were the worst days of her life. She felt she was tricked, when her parents said they were sending her to an academy, she thought," Yippee, an academy, there'll be horses!" She said all the freedom she had growing up in La Conner was gone and she was miserable.

Next is Janet who has crossed my path many times since 2nd grade and we now find we are related by marriage and often share family holidays and picnics. At the end of the row are Danny and Jerry who never left the La Conner area. Danny, who was Rogers's best friend and playmate, took his life in his 40's and Jerry, Roger's cousin, full of promise, died too early from drink and despair.

In the front row little Pat Kirby whose mother taught business classes in the high school, stands next to Max who graduated a year behind us, worked on the Dunlap tugs for years and still lives in La Conner.

Claudette Irvine, shy and quiet, graduated, married, had children but died early. Margaret, with a broad smile is next. In high school we were best friends and practically inseparable. When she married the year after graduation, I was her maid of honor and she was mine in 1956 when Roger and I were married.

And there front and center was the prize winner for beauty and style, Marie Oliver who wore long brown, perfectly coiled curls all done up with a ribbon, every day, not just on picture day. The last time I saw her she was recuperating from cancer and her hair was white and encircled her face in a very becoming pixie style. She was unable to attend our reunion picnic last summer as she was hiking the mountains of Switzerland. Matilda Stone stands next to her.

And there I am, toward the end of the front row between my good friend Karla Ring on one side and my current best friend and husband, Roger Dalan, on the other side. Was that just coincidence? Or was that a choice I made at an early age, to be the one at his side

Comparing the children of 1942 and those of today, I think we look pretty much the same except for our clothing. We had no Nikes, or Adidas, the boys held up their corduroys with suspenders instead of belts, and the girls all wore dresses or little skirts and blouses. No one is wearing an advertisement on their shirt and no Levi's in sight.

Because I Said So

GROWING UP I MOSTLY FOLLOWED the rules my parents had laid out for me, without question, like make your bed, brush your teeth, don't hit your little brother, eat your peas and drink your milk. They knew best, didn't they? But as I became a little worldlier my horizons broadened and I began to question the validity of some of the rules. "But why not" I would plead when denied something. My mother's answer was always, "Because I said so!" End of story.

My mother was a stickler about the manners and appearance of her three little girls and the impressions we made when out in public. Our clothes were clean, dresses freshly ironed and respectfully covering our bottoms. And of course we always had on clean underwear in case there was an accident and we ended up in the hospital. Was that a rule of emergency medicine? Check to make sure the victim is wearing clean underwear? My mother said so and I took it for gospel.

Dorothy, Mary Ann and Janet

Isn't it always the case that when something is forbidden it suddenly becomes more enticing?

When my mother proclaimed, "No daughter of mine is going to get her ears pierced or wear an ankle bracelet! Only gypsies have pierced ears and whores wear ankle bracelets." I was intrigued. I didn't know exactly what whores did for a living but I knew they lived in a house with a red light on the porch and apparently red porch lights were against the law. The ankle bracelet rule must have been a throw-back to the 19th century when society thought it improper for women to show their ankles or any other part of their bodies, hence the long skirts, long sleeves and high necklines on the fashions of that day.

In my teen-age years we shed our bobby socks and saddle shoes for the summer and wore sandals or ballet slippers until school started in the fall. During that time little gold bracelets appeared on girls ankles and if the whole world, and my mother, thought they looked like whores, so be it.

"But why can't we have one?" my sisters and I whined. "Because I said so." was her reply. I never had an ankle bracelet. Never missed it.

Now the pierced ears rule was another story. When a new student walked in to our 6th grade classroom, the first thing I noticed about her was that she had pierced ears. She looked nothing like a gypsy. She had blue eyes, blonde hair, neatly curled, close to her head and wore a pretty little knee length, cotton dress. Everyone knew gypsies had eyes the color of charcoal, long black hair swirling like a raging river down their backs, wore brightly colored, voluminous skirts which dusted the ground as they cavorted through the woods and meadows. Of course they always adorned themselves with flamboyant scarves and jewelry and wore earrings which hung to their shoulders.

WAIT A MINUTE! Have I been lied to? Was this the old bamboozle?

Has my mother ever seen a gypsy? Can Norwegian girls become gypsies? Questions came flying at me like crows in a cornfield. It seemed horribly wrong to doubt the veracity of my mother's rules but this was the proof. This girl looked nothing like a gypsy and here she was wearing pierced earrings like it was simply part of her biological make-up. Imagine my shock when she told us her mother had had it done at the hospital when she was born.

Disillusion and envy swirled around in my mind for weeks. Pierced ears would not make me look like a gypsy, although I rather relished the idea of skipping through La Conner streets in a long peasant skirt covered with beads and bangles and bold jewelry. My mother declared "Not in my lifetime will that ever happen!"

Being an obedient child I waited until I was well into my 40s and had moved way across the continent before I had my ears pierced. As I left the jewelry store that day, my head held high, golden earrings flashing in the sunlight, I could swear I heard violins playing a Hungarian rhapsody.

Only A Dream

I USED TO DREAM THAT when I grew up I would be the next Sonja Henie. She was my idol, this beautiful Norwegian born ice skater with the curly, blonde hair and the alluring smile, who dazzled the world with her twirling and whirling on the ice.

The fact that she had participated in the Olympic Games and come out a champion in the figure skating division was not the most impressive thing in my mind, but the fact that she wore such stunning, sparkling costumes atop her perfectly shaped, beautifully tanned legs which showed off her beguiling white booted skates. That was the thing that fascinated me.

The world fell in love with her on the ice and when she became a leading lady on the movie screen she played to a packed house.

Surely, with practice, I could be just like her, I told myself, as I sat on a bale of straw and laced up my beautiful new white boots with the shining steel blades I was full of hope and confidence but gliding gracefully across the ice didn't come as easily to me as it did to Sonja and after years of frustration and dogged determination I had to face the realization that my dreams would not come true, that Shipstad and Johnson would not be coming down Best Road some magical day, discover me out there in the pasture and sign me up to perform in the glorious Ice Follies extravaganza, due to circumstance far beyond my control.

First of all, I was not skating in a heated, indoor rink maintained by a Zamboni, providing a surface smooth as glass, while gliding in time to the Skaters Waltz on the Wurlitzer. I was skating in a flooded cow pasture with piles of frozen cow manure and stubble poking up through the ice.

All my friends from school were there as well as family and neighbors. I tried my best to perform, to not be the laughing stock of the community. My mother even tried skating, mostly being held up by her brother, Herbert, who was an excellent skater, the kind who moved across the ice, hands clasped behind his back, with long purposeful strides.

And of course I had no coach, only 2 older sisters who didn't know a figure eight from a double Lutz. How was I to learn all the moves? I think I did manage to get the spread-eagle nailed a couple of times though.

I also blame anatomy for my failure to perform. Sonja must surely have been given stronger or perhaps more ankle bones than I seemed to have, for my technique was less than attractive as I slid across the ice with my ankles dragging to the inside.

It would have been great if I could have worn a flirty little short skirt like Sonja but it was freezing cold out there and I looked more like the Michelin Man in long underwear and layer upon layer of heavy clothing, stocking cap and mittens. Where was the glamour?

And last but not least, I blame Global Warming for one year there were no flooded fields and no ice. As the best years of my childhood flew by, ice skating in Skagit County became only a memory.

But there is redemption! I have a beautiful 16 year old granddaughter who also has the love of ice skating in her DNA and who is a sight to behold as her blades dance across the ice in competition and beautiful artistry.

Arielle looks nothing like Sonja for she is tall, with the dark coloring of her Italian father. She started skating at age 5 and after years of hard work and practice, to say nothing of extremely dedicated parents who saw to it that she got to all those early morning lessons, she brings an invigorating spirit and stunning confidence to the ice. I live vicariously through this granddaughter who is a joy to watch.

Out Behind the Barn

Roy Acuff and the Rocky Mountain Boys yodeled their latest sad song, competing with the ever present static blasting from the dusty old radio on the shelf just inside the barn door. The eight or ten cows lined up in the stanchions waiting to be milked, all swished their tails some in time to the music, trying to connect with the swarming flies which did their best to irritate and bother the herd.

This old red, wooden barn, out behind our house was my father's workplace where he could be faithfully found every day of his life, at 6 AM "doing the chores."

Once in the barn he would be met by Barney, our hired man, who had resided on the farm as long as I can remember. He lived in the bunk house down by the slough but ate all his meals at our table. My sisters and I pretty much ignored him all our lives even though we sat next to him at the table. His table manners were gross, he was highly opinionated and not too fond of children. However, he was sober and dependable so he remained.

Barney and my dad both milked the few cows we had and took the shiny steel buckets full of milk to the milk house connected to the barn and poured it into the cooler until the Darigold man came with the tanker truck. One large bucket went directly to the house where my mother would strain it, skim off the cream and fill two big metal pitchers for the refrigerator.

Next the calves would be fed buckets of milk, the horse stalls cleaned and buckets of oats dumped into the feed boxes for the horses. The cows were let out of the barn and the area hosed down. Barn chores were over for the morning and would begin again at 5pm. Now it was time for breakfast and then out to the fields and feed lots where the beef cattle would be tended. Now my dad's work place became our playhouse.

The barn was a wonderful place to play hide and seek for there were many places to hide and sometimes the seeker would just give up before he found you hiding in the grain bin.

One summer my dad poured a large cement slab outside the barn where the cows would wait to be let in, eliminating a lot of the muck and manure which came into the barn.

It was the perfect stage and the area became our theater –in-the round where we performed numerous gala productions. It was hard to round up an audience though and we often had to draft mothers, aunts, cousins and neighbors.

But the best use of the barn came in late spring and early summer when the loft became almost empty waiting for the next hay crop to be harvested and put in the mow. The wood floor under all that hay became the ideal roller skating rink.

We all had skates and were extremely adept at all the moves, frontward, backward, the waltz, we could do it all and we spent hours rolling around to the music of the old radio, cranked up to maximum volume.

One day time slipped away from us and we were still skating and wailing at 5 o'clock when Barney came driving the cows in to milk. Cows can be easily panicked and this was the perfect set of circumstances for them to turn and stampede. He barely escaped with his life and came in yelling and swearing at us. I still remember his threat," If your Dad doesn't give you kids a good thrashing, I'M QUITTING!" he screamed at us.

We didn't even stop to remove our skates but took off across the barnyard to the safety of the house as quickly as we could.

There was no thrashing, for my dad had a sense of humor, but there was a lecture about the timing of barn activities. Barney's threat was just that and he stayed on. In fact he stayed on until long after I was grown and gone. He could be another whole story.

Memories of Bedtime

As I LISTEN TO STORIES about other children and the lives they lived, I realize how different my own childhood was from those where they were indulged, encouraged, and maybe even pampered. Being the third child in a family of four children, I never had the feeling of being special or favored. We all knew who that was.

We learned right from wrong by example, not from nursery rhymes about cute little bunnies and kittens and talking frogs. We had a Mother Goose book which my Mother would sometimes read to us, for to this day those little fantasy rhymes are firmly lodged in my memory's file cabinet. But the bedtime stories which standout so vividly are the ones we devoured when my Dad was in charge of the bedtime routine.

My dad was a rough-neck cowboy, turned farmer and provider when he married and had four children in a matter of a few short years. He was a hard worker, up with the sun and in the fields until dark but always had time to play with us. He was our backyard gymnastic coach who could always beat us in the length of time he could stand on his hands or the number of cartwheels or flips he could do in rapid succession. He had strength and agility well past middle-age, but the most amazing thing about my dad was his memory.

He had a mind that allowed him to read something and remember the details, facts and figures long afterward. Somewhere in his high school years he developed a love of poetry, never writing any of his own but using what he read as something to think about when he was alone in the fields.

His favorite poet was Robert Service who wrote about the lives of men in the Yukon in the days of the Gold Rush. In his youth my dad had owned a volume of these works which was lost by the time he was a father, but it didn't matter, for he had memorized all of them and repeated each one until he owned it.

We always knew when it was his turn to tuck us in at night we would not be hearing any of that prissy stuff about Jack and Jill or Ducky Lucky but real honest to God stuff about the cold, hard realities of life like "The Shooting of Dan McGrew" or "The Cremation of Sam McGee."

My dad loved an audience for his recitations and at bedtime we were willing, captive listeners as he presented these narratives with great expression and style. We heard about the boys who were "whooping it up in the Malamute Saloon, the kid who handled the music box playing a rag time tune." We learned to know "the man at the back of the bar, known as Dangerous Dan McGrew," as well as the love of his life, "the lady known as Lou."

Imagination ruled the night as we pictured being " out in the Great Alone when the moon was awful clear and the icy mountains hemmed you in with a silence you most could hear. With only the howl of a timber wolf as you camped there in the cold, a half dead thing in a stark dead world, clean mad for the muck called gold."

We buried our heads under the covers but hung on every word as he continued, "I ducked my head and the lights went out, and two guns blazed in the dark, a woman screamed, the lights went on and two men lay stiff and stark." Hmmm, stiff and stark. "I think that means dead," I told myself. Dad held our attention and imagination for real life as he introduced us to new vocabulary and we developed an ear for the music of words.

As the years went on we all became so familiar with these poems, we could also recite them. Who needed Mother Goose!

My dad went on to become a member of the Freemasons where he learned to memorize all the rituals and in a few short years progressed through all the stations becoming Grand Master of the local lodge and then on to state level. I'm sure he spent hours in the cab of his tractor reciting all the works for his own enjoyment, to occupy space when he was all alone.

I Didn't Know the
Gun was Loaded

THE SHINY BLACK BUICK, CHROME portholes glinting in the sun, cruised into the Chevron station on Morris Street like a beached whale, carrying the entire Peth family out on a Sunday drive. As the car sidled up to the pumps, Chet, wearing his snappy uniform and customary smile bounded out the door and up to the driver's window. "Fill 'er up, Chet." Dad said through the open window.

While Chet was filling the tank, my dad left the car to do some business inside, perhaps to settle up the bill from the past month, Of course my little brother, who followed my dad wherever he went, tagged along behind. Ever since he was a toddler and big enough to put on his own boots he followed my dad all over the farm, rode with him on the tractor, helped feed the cattle and rode shotgun whenever the truck left the barnyard.

One day he didn't get his boots on fast enough and we watched from the window inside the house as the truck left without him. His little arms flew up in the air, his head reared back, his boots were stomping up and down and he threw himself on the ground in a full blown tantrum, to no avail. My dad hadn't seen him and had left the

farm. Earl was normally endowed with a sweet, quiet manner, stayed out of the way and my dad loved having this little apprentice by his side. With his blonde hair, big blue eyes and sweet disposition, we all adored him.

We waited there in the car on this hot, sultry day so rare in Washington summers, my mother in the front seat and my sisters and I in the back. By some rare luck of the draw, I had a window seat which was unusual. "Open the door, Dorothy. It's hot in here." Janet said. I opened the door but no breeze entered, only the smell of gasoline.

We had been visiting my cousins at their ranch in Bow where most of us had a cousin our same age and had a grand time playing and riding ponies. My cousin Spanky and I had pretended to be cowgirls as we rode the pony double: I was Annie Oakley in a buckskin skirt as we fired the BB gun at imaginary cattle rustlers. She was Dale Evans who could sing all the country songs. She even knew how to yodel and had once sung with a microphone at the 4th of July rodeo in Sedro Wooley. She was awesome.

Now here I was in the car and suddenly noticed the BB gun lying on the floor of the backseat. Without much thought I picked it up and wondered if it was loaded. You should never have a loaded gun in a car. This much I knew. The barrel was warm against my leg as I pointed it out the door and towards the cement driveway. I looked around, there was no one on the sidewalk, no other cars getting gas and I decided the smart thing to do, since I was so concerned about gun safely and the wellbeing of others, would be to discreetly fire the gun at the pavement and find out of it was loaded.

As bad luck would have it, I pulled the trigger at the same instant little brother came sneaking around the car, intending to scare me. He was crouched low to the ground with his little face in perfect alignment with the site on the gun. In horror and surprise I saw the BB hit him in the face. More accurately the mouth.

He screamed, no shrieked, as blood, tears and teeth, mixed with slobber came drooling down his chin. My mom was out of the car in an instant, also screaming and shrieking. "What happened?" she yelled as she viewed me there with the gun in my hand. It was obvious, I thought. Caught red-handed. we immediately all piled in the car and headed for home, my mother cradling Earl's head in her lap, trying to calm him and assess the damage. It appeared I had shot out his front tooth, a brand new permanent one!

"Oooh, You're gonna get it!" Mary Ann whispered in my ear. Like this was something I hadn't thought about! Of course I felt terrible having hurt Earl but I was also concerned about my own hide. I figured I was in for the granddaddy of all spankings. The Nobel prize- winning spanking! Like a convicted felon, I began planning my escape.

The five miles out of town flew by and we were pulling up in front of the house in no time. I threw the car door open and was out like a shot. Faster than a speeding BB. I ran around to the front of the house and down through the orchard, toward the road where I figured I would head north to Canada. However, before reaching the road, I stumbled and fell into a deep, freshly dug ditch. It was deep with a mountain of dirt on each side and a big tile pipe I could sit on so I decided I would hole up there and wait for nightfall to make my escape.

As I sat there in my hiding place I thought about what might be going on in the house. Was Earl still bleeding, still crying? I thought of all the points I could use in self-defense if I was caught. Weren't my parents culpable for letting us have a loaded gun in the car? Why hadn't they checked it or put it in the trunk? I didn't know his face would be there when I pulled the trigger. I didn't mean to shoot him. Accidents happen don't they?

Curiosity got the best of me as the sun began to set and I thought of all possible crawly things that might move in with me as darkness came and I decided to face the music. Which must not have been too bad because I have no memory of the punishment, did not get "skinned alive" or "my hide tanned" which were well-known threats at our house, but I do remember how bad I felt every time Earl smiled and you saw the awful grey cap where his nice white tooth used to be.

When his mouth stopped growing he was able to have a permanent white tooth implanted. I think then he was able to forgive me.

Things My Mother Taught Me

I CAN STILL SEE MY mother standing at the kitchen sink, her faded cotton apron tied around her waist and her arm shoved half way to her elbow, up the chickens' butt.

"Come here Mary Ann and Dorothy, its time you both learned how to clean a chicken." As I recall, we both had better things to do and protested, loudly. I was always the squeamish type but Mary Ann was ten times worse. I was sure she would never be able to do this but I figured I would be okay just watching. Surely she wouldn't actually make us touch the chicken!

"This is something every girl has to know how to do." she said as she slapped the stark naked chicken carcass on the counter. "The hard part has already been done by your dad outside. He put this nice fat hen in boiling water and then plucked all the feathers out. If you see any pin feathers he might have missed you just pull them out." she said. She held up the chicken, stretched out each wing and checked its armpits. I was pretty sure I recognized that chicken who had been happily dancing around the barnyard just yesterday. Who knew it had this sickly, yellow, puckery skin under all those soft, pretty feathers.

"Then you take a sharp knife and cut open the craw, or gullet, and pull out the neck." I hear a strange choking sound beside me and turn to see Mary Ann gagging and looking like she is going to throw up. "Oh, stop that you silly girl, it's just a nice clean chicken, nothing to gag about," she said as she grabbed the hen by the ankles and flipped it over on to its back.

"Now look here, you cut off this little piece where the tail feathers were; that's the butt. Just reach in there like this and pull out all the intestines." she said as she pulled out a glob of guts and dropped them in the metal dish pan. More gagging. "This is the liver and these are the lungs, throw them away. Save the heart and the gizzard. You know your dad loves the gizzard."

Gizzards, heart, lungs and liver. "Call them what you want, I think, but if it comes out of the inside of that chicken, it's guts." No one should eat guts! "I'm never eating chicken again as long as I live!" vowed Mary Ann. My mother always made the most delicious fried chicken so I was pretty sure I couldn't just give that up but I was also pretty sure that I would never ever be the one to gut a chicken!

My sister and I talked about this years later and Mary Ann said, "Do you suppose she didn't know that you could buy chicken at the store, already cleaned and cut up?" I know I have lived to this ripe old age without ever putting this chicken cleaning lesson to use. I let Mr. Tyson take care of all the dirty work.

The Sack Man

As a child I had many fears. No one ever called me Braveheart! Living on a farm with all sorts of animals might seem like paradise to many children but they don't know how overwhelming it can be. I always felt like I didn't belong there among all those terrifying animals. Maybe the stork accidentally dropped me on his way to an animal free zone.

The monstrous work horses had feet like massive hammers which could crush a small child who happened to be in the way as they came clomping into the barn. Riding horses, especially Shetland ponies, could go galloping off with you on their backs, then feel frisky and buck you off, leaving you stranded far from home. They also have very large, sharp teeth which they can use to bite you, leaving bleeding holes in your arms or legs.

Those mean, beady-eyed chickens sitting on their nests like prima donnas, just waiting for a little girl to come gather eggs, could peck holes in your hands with those needle-like beaks. And cows look harmless enough but, don't ever walk too close to one in a stanchion waiting to be milked. They can kick those hind legs out and send you right out of the barn with those sharp hooves. Their tails are also used as whips and can sting you on arms and face, leaving red welts.

All the animals on the farm scared me but my biggest fear came not from an animal but a man! The SACK MAN was the one! I suppose he had a name, but we never knew it. To us he became the dreaded SACK MAN.

Every couple of months the SACK MAN arrived on the scene in a dark, panel truck with no windows in the back and he came to sell my dad gunny sacks. When you raise oats and potatoes and ship to market, gunny sacks are a big part of farm life. They are also good to have around if you're going to have sack races at the family picnic.

The short, roly-poly little Jewish man who spoke loudly and with a thick accent which sounded so foreign to all of us here in waspish Skagit County struck fear into my little girls heart. His brazen manner would often startle us as he came waddling into the house unannounced, wearing a three piece suit, shiny black shoes and a silly little tam sort of hat upon his head. He sure didn't look like a farmer.

Because he appeared so different, I became quite suspicious and fearful of the man, especially after we were told by my parents that he kidnapped bad little girls, put them in gunny sacks which he threw in the back of that dark, windowless truck and hauled them off to the city where they were never seen again.

With childish gullibility and trusting every word my parents spoke as gospel, I bought the story, hook, line and sinker. The threat," The SACK MAN will get you" became the number one fear in my life. I doubt that Dr. Spock would have recommended this as a good parenting technique but it straightened me right up.

Early on I learned to recognize his truck and as soon as I spotted it pull into the barnyard, I did the Houdini and disappeared. I had several good hiding places on the farm; inside I headed for the bunk beds where the bottom bunk rested so close to the floor I had to slither like a snake on my belly to get under it. No way could a fat little SACK MAN squirm under there.

An underground bunker where seed potatoes, dusted with lime, waited in storage, made a great hiding place if you could stand the smell. No one would ever think of looking for me in the potato pit! In the center of the pit stood a long wooden makeshift table with sharp knives attached to four stations where workers would slice the seed potatoes. In a desperate situation I could probably rip one of those knives off to defend myself.

Another favorite place to hide if I could manage to sneak across the barnyard to the old red barn and up into the hay mow without being seen, I could lie comfortably on that soft fragrant pillow of hay until his truck left the property.

Due to divine intervention or my own utter cleverness or perhaps plain good luck, I was never kidnapped by the SACK MAN nor were either of my sisters.

When I grew up and left the farm far behind, while living in the Chicago area, I worked with a girl, Mary, who was born and raised in the city. As she told me about her childhood one day, she said her mother had threatened her with "Farmer Brown", an old man dressed in jeans and an old straw hat, who came around the streets in her neighborhood selling fresh vegetables. Her mother told her "Farmer Brown" kidnapped bad little girls and took them away to the farm and forced them to stay there.

I thought, "What a funny coincidence, we are all a little fearful and prejudiced about the unfamiliar or different ones we meet."

A Pleasurable Scent

EVERY SPRING WHEN MOST HOMEOWNERS in Skagit County get back on their riding lawnmowers and begin that regular Saturday morning routine where they cut the grass around their home and send that delicious scent wafting into the air, I am transported back to my fourth grade classroom at LaConner Elementary school. The room was on the north side of the building where a full wall of windows climbed to the ceiling providing a panoramic view of the playfield and the bus garage. The windows were open wide.

I sat at my desk, feet flat on the floor, right elbow slightly off the edge of the desk, pencil placed properly between thumb and forefinger and resting on tall man, I slid my arm back and forth, back and forth, across the lined paper as effortlessly and smooth as a marshmallow cloud floating across the sky.

No, that's not me making line after line of perfectly formed O' s which would earn me an A in this Penmanship class. I'm the one sitting in the next row, clutching my pencil like the "jaws of life", teeth clenched and perspiration dripping from my brow as I silently plead with my muscles to cooperate and form a perfect O. Just one row before the Penmanship Nazi comes with that lethal ruler. "Please."

Suddenly, something changed. I sensed a feeling of calm wash over me like the ocean rushing upon the shore. My shoulders relaxed, I laid my pencil down in the little groove at the top of the desk, closed my eyes and took a deep, deep breath. That delicious scent of new mown grass floated through my consciousness bringing me peace.

Then I heard the sound of the gang mower and knew Johnny Rock was out there doing his job. Looking around the room I saw the teacher was busy harassing another uncoordinated student and I made my move. Quickly and almost silently I glided toward the window where the pencil sharpener awaited the clever time- wasters and faux pencil sharpeners. I inserted my pencil and began grinding it into sawdust.

To be able to smell the scent more clearly through the open window and also see school janitor, Johnny Rock out there on our playfield, bouncing along on the tractor seat like he is sitting on a cushion of Jello, pulling the double-barrel gang mower behind him while little blades of grass scatter into the air filled me with pleasure as I stood at the window. The melodious rumble of the mower lulled me into a trance. I took a deep breath and closed my eyes.

"Dorothy, get back to your seat!" Miss Peterson's shrill voice interrupted my reverie and I scurried back to my desk.

Working for a Living

I WENT TO WORK AT the age of 10. Picking strawberries was not my first choice as a career path but then I had no path of my own, just blindly followed the path chosen by my two older sisters before me.

Fortunately, I met all the qualifications of the job; I had reached the magic age of 10 when you no longer cry for your mother when things go terribly wrong, I was breathing, had ten fingers, all in working order, could crawl through weeds, mud and rain, and knew the difference between a dirt clod and a strawberry.

It was an entry level position, low pay and no, I mean NO benefits. I was told there was room for advancement to Apprentice Picker and then with time and experience maybe all the way to Checker which was the ultimate position for you never had to crawl down a row again but would sit in the shade of a big beach umbrella sipping a cold Coca Cola while the pickers were sweating in the afternoon sun.

Working conditions were deplorable! Like postal workers, nothing, but nothing, not rain, thunder and lightning nor blinding snow could keep us from our appointed route down the rows of berries. Our work day started early, before the sun rose above the mountains and the dew was still on the berry vines, which meant your fingers were wet and freezing, icicles under your fingernails and shirt sleeves wet up to your elbows.

Usually by noon the sun would appear, the clouds would all run away and the temperature would climb to sun stroke level without so much as a hint of shade anywhere for miles. If you were so smart as to have brought a big straw hat you could have sold it and made more money than you made picking berries.

After a couple of short weeks on the job, the fun seemed to have disappeared and even the thought of future wealth on payday lost its luster. I began to whine like a two year old when my Dad woke me up on a work day morning. Oh, and by the way, every day was a work day. Strawberries do not ripen only on weekdays, much to my dismay, they ripen every day and have to be picked before they rot on the vine. Someone should have told me this fact of life.

I feigned illness. Maybe my ankle was broken, I thought I had a fever, maybe measles. I moaned and groaned, whined and whimpered but my Dad saw right through my flim-flam act and I was out the door, lunch pail in hand to another day on the job.

One year my little brother, Earl and cousin Buzzy also thought it would be fun to pick berries for a living although I don't think they were 10 yet. They spent the first day sitting on their carriers, in one spot eating berries by the handful. At the end of the day they were fired. I pretended not to know them.

There was a lesson to be learned in my first summer employment and it was about commitment. I had signed up for the job, assuring the owner that I would stay for the duration of the berry season and would then qualify for the bonus. I looked for a way to override the bonus but my Dad assured me there was none.

How I looked forward to 4th of July that year when the berries became smaller and fewer and we were getting close to the season end and I would retire.

I grew up a little that summer. I learned that whining does no good in the "work-a-day world." No one listens, no one cares. The payoff for hard, miserable work comes on payday when for the first time in your life you have your own money. And a pocket full of independence.

It was so long ago I became a worker, I can't remember what I spent my earnings on, probably candy bars and bubble gum but at the end of the season I was already looking forward to next year when I would be right back out there crawling through the berry patch and hanging in there for the bonus.

A Surprise in the Night

IT WAS MORNING ON A school day and the smell of coffee floated upstairs through the black iron floor grate. I could hear Janet and Mary Ann in the next room discussing the day's activities and what they would wear. I dressed quietly in my own room and hurried out the door and down the rickety, moss-covered steps and into the back door of the house where water was boiling furiously in a large rocking pot on the monstrous black and chrome wood stove for our oatmeal breakfast. Hot oatmeal was the first course of our usual hardy, weekday breakfast. Thick sliced bacon which was sizzling and spitting in the old cast iron skillet would accompany eggs, potatoes and toast for the second course.

All children were checked for clean faces, brushed teeth and combed hair and swished out the door to wait for the school bus, leaving my mother free to have a second cup of coffee and plan the next meal. At 12 o'clock, noon, the men would come in from the fields and expect to be served a full, hot dinner which most certainly would include meat, potatoes, gravy, vegetables and homemade dessert or fruit.

We headed off for school that day, with no idea of the surprise which was in store for us that night.

After school we had a snack and did our chores, the most important being filling the bottomless wood box on the back porch to insure the old Monarch would continue to belch out heat for a multitude of delicious meals and baked goods.

That night after supper, my dad went out with the truck and had not returned by bedtime. I remember being awakened from a deep sleep by my mother who excitedly told us to get up and come into the kitchen and discover the surprise our Dad had for us.

When all sleepy-eyed children were assembled in the kitchen, the back door opened slightly and we could see our Dad out on the porch struggling with something which was kicking against the wall. Then he lifted the thing and stepped through the darkened night into the light of the kitchen with a small red pony in his arms. All four tiny legs were hanging down over his arms as he held the pony's belly close to his. Then he unceremoniously stood him right down on the linoleum floor as all four of us children jumped up and down, squealing, laughing and shouting, "A pony, a pony!"

In the background, my mother was shouting,

"George, get that horse out of my kitchen!" but nobody seemed to hear her as we all crowded around the shaggy- maned Shetland pony who would become our friend, companion and nemesis for years and years!

My First Ride

MY FIRST RIDE WAS NOT a car but a Shetland pony. I was about five when she came into our lives, much to our surprise. My dad carried the little red pony with the shaggy, bushy, bronze colored mane, into the house in his arms and I thought we must surely be the luckiest kids in the world! Isn't that every kids dream? To have a pony? If I'd known then, what I know now, I would have said, "Be careful what you wish for."

We named her Trixie (Mistake #1) thinking we would teach her a few tricks like taking a bow, dancing to music, coming when you called her name, simple things like that. I pictured myself at rodeos giving awesome performances on the back of my famous pony. I would be dressed in a snazzy costume, all satin and sequins and shiny white boots as I raced around the ring doing death-defying tricks like the shoulder stand, the rear fender back bend or the suicide drag while waving the American flag. (Mistake #2)

We spent hours in the barn getting to know Trixie and her us. We also spent hours grooming her. When someone suggested we get rid of that wild, bushy mane, out came the clippers and soon she looked like the Fuller Brush man had stopped by and installed sharp, pointy bristles from her ears down to her back. (Mistake #3)

Trixie was supposedly broke to ride when my dad bought her but she was definitely lacking in etiquette and had apparently never heard that old proverb, "Never bite the hand that feeds you."

Catching her took at least two riders, three was better. One of us would carry the bridle, hidden discreetly behind the back, while the other made clicking or coaxing noises while offering a handful of oats. She was smart enough to go for the oats and then bite the hand that fed her, leading to crying, disappointment and another failed attempt to catch her. Even though she was just a little pony, she had teeth as sharp as Ginzu knives and when she curled her top lip back and flashed them at you, you'd better run for cover.

Although we spent months trying to build up a relationship with Trixie, one of trust and mutual respect, it just didn't work out. We hadn't expected her to be so stubborn and I think she just didn't like us. We quickly learned not to take our eyes off her when leading her to the barn, for her favorite trick was to bite you in the back, and while you were hopping around in pain, she would rub that wire-bristled mane against you, removing at least one layer of skin.

My dad bought us a pretty little saddle for her and with help I could get it on her ornery little body, but usually rode her bareback. In the summer I often rode bareback with shorts instead of long pants which caused my warm sweaty legs to be covered with horsehair. Just one of the hazards of being a trick rider! We never got around to teaching Trixie any tricks but she had a few of her own. One of her favorites was the manner in which she could get me off her back.

My best friend Marilyn lived just across the road from us, down a long lane, which was lined on both sides by barbed wire fence. I would ride Trixie across the road at a trot, thinking I was in control and as soon as we got inside the lane, between those two barbed wire fences, she would lift up all four legs and like a Lipizzaner, would do a horizontal move into the ditch, snuggling my bare legs up next to the barbed wire and race forward like Seabiscuit, removing the skin from my leg.

I don't know if I was a slow learner or if I just had too much trust in that ruthless pony, but she did this to me over and over again. Coming home she would jump the other way so I usually walked around with two scarred legs all summer.

I remember one day my sister, Mary Ann was trotting around the yard on Trixie when that devious little pony decided she'd had enough and quickly darted under the apple tree scraping her rider off on a low slung branch. The result was a broken arm for my sister and satisfaction for Trixie.

Trixie grew up and so did we and one day our feet almost touched the ground as we rode so we passed her on to one of our unsuspecting cousins who thought it would be wonderful to have a Shetland pony. As evil as Shetlands are, they do have a long life so she must have had many more years in Skagit County making other children's lives miserable.

Sisters Mary Ann and Janet riding double on Trixie

Innocent 'Till Proven Guilty

HAVE YOU EVER BEEN FALSELY accused? You read about it every day in the Skagit Valley Herald. The wife is found dead at the bottom of the stairs, the husband is arrested, lawyers up and pleads NOT GUILTY.

Thousands of dollars are missing from the foundation account and Madam President of the organization, claiming she had nothing to do with it, pleads NOT GUILTY. It could be true, for once it happened to my sister Mary Ann and me. We were falsely accused.

For weeks we had been looking forward to the annual Fall Festival held at Fredonia Grange. It was something we did as a family each year. We were not Grange members but many of our neighbors were so we were sure to see many friends and acquaintances there as we took part in a wide range of activities. My mother, of course had brought a pie to be entered in the baking contest and my dad liked visiting with local farmers, some he had known all his life. The thing that interested us the most however, was the chance to win prizes at all the game booths.

As we entered the hall, people were talking and laughing, kids were chasing each other around spilling bags of popcorn on the old wooden floor while somewhere in the background loud country music was bouncing off the walls. Sensory overload splashed in my face and I couldn't decide where to go first.

Mary Ann surveyed the room with a glance, trying to locate a game she knew she could win and what the prizes would be. She was tall for her age, with long arms and legs and self-confidence riding on her broad shoulders.

She had developed an arm that could have put her in the major leagues at age 12 and she knew she was a winner while I was pretty sure the only prize I could win was at the fish pond where the man behind a backdrop would place some dinky little prize on every line. I would stick to my sister like glue hoping she would share her loot with me.

"Liddle girls, step right up. Try your luck at putting the ball through the pumpkin's mouth." A huge orange pumpkin, made of metal was suspended on the wall at the back of the booth where the barker was shouting at prospective players. "Give it a try, just look at the prizes." he said holding out his hand with a baseball in it. With his other hand he pulled a big square red bandana handkerchief out of the back pocket of his overalls just in time to catch a loud sneeze. Looking past this poor man who was obviously suffering from a cold we saw the wall behind the pumpkin which was covered from floor to ceiling with hundreds of jars of hard candy. They were quart jars sparkling like jewels with every kind of colorful, delicious candy inside.

There were brightly colored ribbon candies, burgundy sugared raspberry filled, clear as glass rock candy, silky striped peppermint straws and every other candy you ever dreamed of. Now this was a prize worth trying for. Without a moment's hesitation, Mary Ann gave the germ-laden man her ticket and reached for the baseball. She would have three chances to put a ball through the smiling face of the pumpkin.

I watched, full of hope as MaryAnn took the first ball in her hand and squinting at the pumpkin, wound her arm around in a circle as if she were on the pitcher's mound in Yankee Stadium and let it fly. .With a clang and a bang she hit the pumpkin just above his left eye. The noise was heard around the hall and a crowd of spectators began to appear. "I was just warming up," she announced to the crowd. She took the second ball and adding a little grandstanding for the crowd, threw it right through the smile of that pumpkin.

People cheered and the surprised barker said, "Good for you, Honey. Now you can have 81 of those jars of candy." Mary Ann and I looked at each other with our mouths wide open. We couldn't believe our ears! Mary Ann grabbed me by the collar and drug me back to the wall of candy. "81 jars, can you believe it, she said. You will have to help me. We can never carry that many, we'll only take about 12. Hold out your arms and I'll load you up."

People were lining up at the booth after seeing such a successful winner and the sneezy barker had his hands full taking tickets, laying down the rules and wiping his nose, while we filled our arms with candy jars.

"Hold on," he yelled when he turned toward the wall and saw us taking all his candy. The Grange Master, High Potentate or whatever he was called happened to be walking by the booth at just that moment and the barker flagged him down and shouted," These girls are stealing all my candy."

False accusation! We stopped dead in our tracks, jars of candy piled up in our arms from our waists to our chins. "You said we could have 81 jars, and we're only taking about 12." "You're crazy, he shouted, I said anyone."

We were so embarrassed! But it was much better than being thrown into jail and we moved on down the midway to the next game, enjoying our candy as we went.

Off Limits

Growing up on the farm was the epitome of running wild and free. Darkness and hunger were the only things that forced me inside. With imagination as vast as the western sky and as deep as Puget Sound, I spent the day outside playing wherever I wanted as long as I stayed off the road and out of the bunkhouse.

The bunkhouse was a small square building in disrepair with two curtain-less, dirty windows on the north side, and a bulky wooden door in between, at the top of three or four rickety steps. It was heated by a wood stove and had no indoor plumbing. It was void of style and color and appeared to have stood in that spot in the barnyard for at least a hundred years To Barney, our hired man, it was home, his inner sanctum and definitely off limits to my sisters and me.

I can't remember a time when Barney wasn't there so maybe he came to the farm before I arrived on the scene in 1935. He came from a dirt poor family with 10 kids in some little back woods town upriver. He was tall, and thin as a ten penny nail. His teeth were rotten and some were missing but it didn't matter much, for he seldom smiled. His face always clean shaven, with skin as lined and tough as leather, had one redeeming quality; his clear, sky blue eyes.

Sunday was his day off and he usually went to visit his family or fishing with his brother. He had a nice little boat he would load into his pickup and take for these fishing trips. During the week the boat was parked beside the bunkhouse on a slope leading down to the slough.

"Make sure those damn kids stay out of my boat," he'd tell my dad. But what kid could resist the temptation to go floating down the stream on a lovely day when no one was around. We couldn't go far but we did have some fun times in that nice little boat.

Just like a member of the family, he joined us at the table, breakfast, dinner and supper, six days of the week. He never complained about the food, but why should he; my mother was an excellent cook. He ate with gusto and atrocious table manners. I was always embarrassed when a friend joined us for a meal. He shoveled food into his mouth like a pig at the trough and chewed with his mouth open all the while relating the events of his last hunting trip.

We never knew if Barney had a life-long acute sinus condition or just a bad habit of sniffing, no, snorting, where he would suck up one huge breath and phlegm would come rattling up from somewhere deep inside. Each time he did it, he drowned out all conversation. It was a disgusting sound. Blowing his nose would have been preferable and we always gave him a multi-pac of big red bandana/handkerchiefs for Christmas but he never got the hint.

Barney always felt entitled to voice his opinion regarding our schooling, grades, behavior/ activities and punishment, which endeared him to no one.

He smoked and rolled his own cigarettes at the table, spilling his Prince Albert tobacco all over my mother's immaculate floor. She suffered in silence.

Dad taught us to treat him with respect, (though it was hard), and recognize his right to privacy by never entering the bunkhouse. When I left home at 21 years of age, he was still there.

Although I broke lots of rules growing up, I can honestly say, I never entered the bunkhouse.

Slopping the Hogs

OF ALL THE MODERN CONVENIENCES I have in my kitchen, the one I am fondest of is my garbage disposal. I would surrender the microwave or the dishwasher before I would give up my disposal. I hate garbage or more precisely, I hate dealing with it. This could be a result of the dysfunctional relationship I had with the outrageous table scraps as a child.

At the end of each day the galvanized bucket under the kitchen sink, containing egg shells, potato peelings, coffee grounds, onion skins, orange peelings, meat scraps and God knows what else, had to be emptied. We called it SLOP and it went to the pigs. Those greedy, gluttonous pigs.

The unlucky child chosen to empty the slop would take the bucket out to the pig pen, dump it into the trough and bring it back empty. Pretty straight forward. By clever design, I usually avoided the task for several reasons: #1. It was usually dark, #2. The bucket was heavy #3 It smelled BAD and #4 I was scared of those snarling, snorting, squealing swine!

When I WAS drafted for SLOP detail, I usually misjudged my distance in the dark and the slop landed outside the pen and the bucket landed inside. Disastrous! Someone would have to get in the pen and retrieve the bucket.

The pigs, maybe three fat, pink sows and one old cantankerous hog, were housed in the distant back corner of the yard in a sturdy pen built of rough fence posts, with a wide food trough next to the fence and a lean-to for protection from the weather. They were fat, noisy, slobbering animals that rolled around in the mud all day and had no redeeming qualities as far as I could tell. I never made the connection pig/bacon, pork chop/hog. In fact I never connected the animals walking around on the farm to the food on my plate. Life was better that way.

Mary Ann, my middle sister, was usually the one who slopped the pigs. I don't know why, maybe she volunteered. She would have been the one who would do that. I cannot remember a time when she misbehaved, was belligerent or sassy, or ever got into trouble. Well there was that one time she threw the cat out the upstairs window but that was a science project to see if cats do always land on their feet. They do and the cat seemed to be none the worse for wear after the fall.

Mary Ann was always good natured, eager to help. Janet and I were not. We were pretty sure Mary Ann was the favorite child. I can see why. I couldn't see it then but now I understand.

Mary Ann was also different in stature than the rest of us Peths, who were built like fire plugs; stocky and close to the ground. She was long and lean with the body of an athlete. She was so limber she could walk on her hands as well as her feet, do cartwheels till the cows came home and she was beauty in motion when she went to slop the hogs. With long, purposeful strides, the bucket swinging from one arm, she moved gracefully across the back porch, down the steps and across the lawn. Swiftly, she glided past the swing set, on by the pump house, behind the playhouse to the pig pen where she effortlessly tossed the slop over the fence and into the trough of the delighted pigs. Just as swiftly, through the dark of night, she would return to the house with the bucket in hand. Easy, peasey.

I do recall once, however, when she didn't do such a good job of slopping the hogs. She was headed toward the pig pen one dark night, a full bucket of slop hanging at her side, when a dark figure stepped out from behind the pump house, stopping her in her tracks. She screamed and let the bucket fly, slop and all.

My uncle Herbert, who was my mother's brother, lived on a dairy farm just through the field from us and would often stroll over for a visit in the evening when all his chores were done. He was a great practical joker and enjoyed popping up unexpectedly to frighten someone. Well, I remember he wore the slop that night.

The Occurrence

IT WAS IN 4TH GRADE when my big opportunity occurred; my moment in the sun, so to speak. Spelling had always been easy for me. It seemed I had inherited my father's amazing memory for after a few minutes of study each week; I got 100% on every spelling test. Now, after nearly a whole year of classroom spelling bees, even bees against 5th and 6th graders, I was a winner. Being one of two 4th graders chosen to be in the countywide spelling bee was probably the most exciting thing that had ever occurred in my young life.

When I awoke that morning, I could hardly believe the day had finally arrived. Everything had been planned the night before; my hair was washed and curled, I would wear my bright blue puffy dress, a matching ribbon in my hair and my patent leather Mary Jane's, which I wore only to Sunday school and on special occasions. It was my special day and everyone would know it.

Somehow I survived the morning and in the afternoon boarded the bus with the other students for the trip to Mt.Vernon and the radio station, KBRC, where the event would take place.

"I before e, except after c or when sounded as "a" in neighbor or weigh" I was repeating over and over to myself in a barely audible voice. Those sitting around me were wondering, "Is she okay?" "Drop the final e before adding a suffix, double the final consonant before adding a suffix beginning with a vowel." I had to remember all the rules if I was to become the champion today.

Being the third girl in the family, I was forever trying to prove myself in the race against those two older sisters. But I always came in last. Today would be the day! I would show the world.

I could spell upside down and backwards. As a champion speller and winner of the spelling bee, I imagined my picture on the front page of the Puget Sound Mail, the Skagit Valley Herald and maybe even the Seattle Times.

As I stepped up to the microphone in the first round, I wore confidence like a crown. "Receive, R-E-C-E-I-V-E, receive." I said matter- of- factly.

People were eliminated one by one; some crying, some sobbing, some screaming foul and some demanding a "do over" but rules were rules. Suddenly there were only two remaining; me and Margaret Sampson.

"Occurrence, there was a strange occurrence on Main Street this morning." the announcer said. Silence filled the studio. The only sound was the beating of my frantic heart, which everyone could hear. "Please let that be

Margaret's word." PLEASE! Silence paraded around the room like the high school marching band. Dead air from KBRC. "Dorothy, the announcer said, it is your word, would you like it repeated?"

"Yes," I responded, hoping time would somehow help. As everyone watched, all the spelling rules joined hands and walked right out of the room. And that crown of confidence rolled off my curly little head right onto the floor. "O-C-C-U-R-E-N-C-E, occurrence?" I said. "I'm sorry," the announcer responded.

All the starch left my body and I wilted onto my chair like a dead petunia. There were no tears but it was obvious I was embarrassed, angry and disappointed. It was definitely not my finest hour, especially as I watched Margaret spell occurrence with two R's and become the 4th grade champion.

Although it seemed a possibility at the time, the stars did not fall from the sky, the birds did not stop singing, the world did not come to a screeching halt because of that long ago Spelling Bee and I am still considered a master speller by my family.

It's What's for Dinner

IT HAS BEEN ABOUT 70 years since I last tasted liver and it hasn't been long enough. I can still taste it.

Coming to the table on liver days, I knew what to expect. The smell of liver and onions was enticing, however the taste was terrible on my palate. But I knew I would be forced to eat a small portion. You see my home was not a democracy. Parents ruled and kids had no vote. I thought this form of government was totally unfair and longed to protest with a walkout or march up and down the driveway with a picket sign thereby alerting Skagit County to the unfair practices going on within, but I lacked the necessary courage.

Terror filled my heart when I walked into the kitchen and saw that horrible mound of bloody innards lying on the counter. I knew it was either liver day or someone had recently been murdered here. How could my mother stand to touch it? I had actually seen her pick up the disgusting glob of guts with her bare hands, dredge it in flour and plop it into the frying pan. How could she!

Living on a cattle ranch of course we butchered and ate our own beef. Each time this occurred the poor animal surrendered one bloody mass of liver probably weighing four or five pounds, which meant it would show up on our table frequently.

For some reason, which I never understood, my parents seemed to love it. I can even remember sitting in a booth in some local diner and after what seemed like an eternity as they poured over the many choices on the menu, would order liver and onions. What! When you could have anything? At least I never had to eat it at a restaurant.

I guess my mother somehow knew we all needed regular servings of liver to get our necessary iron requirements. Perhaps that ugly little cod liver oil pill we were forced to swallow each day wasn't enough. I don't know if that little yellow pill was made up of cod or liver but it tasted horrible, I distinctly remember.

In our non-democratic household my mother was the one who decided what we would eat, whether we liked it or not. She put that platter of liver and onions on the table and it was "What's for dinner." Choice crumbled and fell apart like a cornbread muffin.

When our daughter was raising her two children I often observed the breakfast, lunch and dinner routine where she would ask each one what they wanted to eat and then like a short order cook in a diner would fill their request. What kind of permissive child rearing was this? It wasn't how she was raised.

A cousin told me of asking her three year old son recently, "What should we have for dinner tonight, Rory?" After some serious thought he replied, "How 'bout frosting." Sounds good to me but we can't let children make those kinds of decisions, can we? I guess that's why parents make the rules and kids end up eating liver.

When raising my children I was probably too insistent that they eat certain foods but I can honestly say I never made them eat liver, because it never came into our house. Never. And we all survived.

Everyone Deserves
a Chance to Fly

PENGUINS, CHICKENS AND EMUS ARE all birds which come equipped with wings, however they do not fly. The Washington State Lottery Commission however, thinks they must want to fly so their commercial shows them being harnessed under a hang glider and soaring over rolling hills, probably in California since it's kind of a nutty thing to do.

First we see the harnessed-up flyer in a jumpsuit tromping up a small hill with the penguin eagerly waddling along behind. Then we see them airborne, the penguin in a harness, hanging beneath the belly of the pilot with his little arms stretched out to his side, a smile on his face, enjoying the ride.

Next we see a big fluffy white chicken doing the same thing while a few other chickens are waiting on the ground for their turn.

The surprise comes when we see the pilot open the gate to the holding pen and lead a BIG, BIG bird out on a rope. It's an emu! His long skinny legs flop around as he follows the pilot up the hill. His eagerness is apparent and his immense golden eyes are afire with excitement. He flies away in a sling attached to a hang glider on each side.

"Every bird should get to fly," the announcer says. "Whose world could you change?" All you have to do is buy a lottery ticket.

The commercial reminded me of the time I flew over the slough on our farm. I was about 4 years old and was out playing by myself in the barnyard. It was a blustery, windy day and as I ran down the hill toward the slough, arms out to the side, little grey coat flying out behind me, I suddenly felt my feet leave the ground.

I kept running, through the field of buttercups and down to the water's edge. A gust of wind rushed under my small body, filling my coat with air, my senses flooded with imagination and I was soaring over the slough. I could hardly believe it. I was flying!

I know now I should have kept the miracle to myself. But I couldn't contain myself and blurted it out to my mother and dad and all the hired men who were having dinner at our house that day. They were all duly impressed and wanted all the details. No one questioned the veracity of my story. I became overwhelmed with all the attention it brought me and went on to tell my sisters when they came home from school. "Did you know I can fly?" I asked everyone who stopped at our house that day.

They say that sometimes when you tell a lie so many times, you start to believe it and that's what happened to me. To this day friends and relatives sometimes remark, "Say, Dorothy, do you remember that day you flew over the slough?" Of course I do, everyone deserves a chance to fly!

Janet and the Fire Drill

I WAS BORN THE THIRD child in our family. The fact that I was the third girl must have been a major disappointment to my dad who was a farmer and would rather have had sons. A farmer needs sons to help with the work in the fields and barns, to milk the cows and feed the horses. In some families daughters fill those positions but not on our farm. It was "man's work."

My oldest sister was Janet. She was 3 and a half years older than I. Next was Mary Ann who was 15 months younger than Janet. They were close in age and comradery. Janet was definitely the leader of the group and MaryAnn and I looked up to her, partly because she was older but also because she had such self-confidence and the personality of a leader. She enjoyed her position as ringleader.

I remember one day when I was probably about 7, the three of us came home from school and found our mother was gone. This happened occasionally and we knew we were supposed to change from school clothes to play clothes, have a snack and do our chores; the first being to carry wood from the woodshed and fill the wood box on the back porch.

Well, Janet had big plans for us that day so we quickly changed clothes and then she told us we were going to have a "fire drill."

I think it was Fire Prevention Week and her class had been discussing fire safety at school. But she was either confused about the procedure or just decided to embellish a bit to make things more exciting for us.

We lived in a small frame house with 2 bedrooms, a large kitchen with a big wood stove and a small living room which contained an oil-fired stove. On the front of the house a wide porch overlooked the apple orchard. It was an old house and my mother always worried about fire. It seemed to me she had an unreasonable fear of fire which she somehow managed to pass on to all of us.

Janet reasoned that she would be happy to come home and find us having a "fire drill." I was hesitant. It sounded like a lot of work to me. But Janet was convincing, she could have sold ice cubes to Eskimos. She began barking out orders and stressing how important speed was.

First I took my dolls and toys and books and carried them out to the front porch. Janet shouted, "No. No. That's too close to the house. Take everything out to the yard and put it in a big pile." Mary Ann and I loaded our arms with our most prized possessions and ran out to the yard. "Hurry, hurry, she yelled "the house is on fire!" We were having such fun!

When most of our toys were outside we started on the clothes. "Grab the kitchen chairs," she said, seeing we needed someplace to pile the clothing. All she needed was a megaphone as she barked out orders like a circus ringmaster.

Quickly we finished hauling all of our own things out as Janet assured us we were doing a great job and next we should go to our parent's room and try to save all their things. "Mama will be so happy," she told us.

She couldn't have been more wrong!!

In a few minutes we had my mother's nice dresses, still on hangers, draped over chairs on the lawn. Everything was helter-skelter. A mountain of toys, dolls, furniture, shoes, boots and clothes stood in the middle of the yard when we saw an ominous cloud of dust and that great, old black Buick came rolling into the barnyard and stopped next to the sidewalk to the house.

I remember the look of astonishment on my mother's face. I can't recall all of the consequences but I'm pretty sure "Mama wasn't happy"!!And it was no fun at all putting everything back. I don't recall if Janet took the blame, but I doubt it.

Janet went on to be a leader in many other ways. In high school she was THE cheerleader and I always thought she was truly in her element wearing a flirty little costume, a megaphone in her hand shouting out the cheers for the spectators.

Sunday Drive

GOING FOR A RIDE IN the car on Sunday afternoon was a traditional event in my family. Perhaps there were times when this was a good thing but I mostly remember the times when it was not.

We always had a nice big car, usually a Buick, with plenty of room for my two sisters and me in the backseat. My brother, the little prince who would one day inherit the kingdom, usually rode in front between my parents.

Those Sunday drives, confined in that close space, for what seemed like hours, seemed to bring out the worst in the three of us girls and we would end up in trouble for fighting. It was either pinching, pulling hair, Indian wrist burns, finger bending or maybe even biting. And then the crying, whining and tattling until my dad would begin his threats of punishment.

When all else failed and he had reached his limit of tolerance he would haul the old Buick off to the side of the road, turn around and tell us, "Okay, girls get out of the car. You can walk from here and see how you like that!"

Usually by the time we got to this point we were near enough to see our house down the road and it wasn't too far to walk. Janet and Mary Ann were both older and bolder and jumped out of the car, eager to walk the rest of the way but I was always afraid.

I was afraid of the dark, afraid of cars which might come along with kidnappers in them. Afraid of the boogey man who might also be walking home that night. I remember leaping down into the ditch whenever head-lights approached. In a few minutes we would be home, none the worse for wear and receiving the lecture about how to behave on the Sunday drive, after which we vowed to be good next time.

In the early 40's my dad, like most adults, was curious about the war and longed for information on what was happening. You could only gath-er so much info from the radio and the movie newsreels so he liked our Sunday drives to take us to points near the Naval Air Base on Whidbey Island where maybe we could watch for Japs who might be flying in to drop a bomb on us.

One Sunday we headed south on Highway 99 to Seattle where we vis-ited the Ballard Locks. Perhaps my dad thought the Japs might be coming by sea. Maybe we could spot an enemy submarine.

The drive had been long, the day was hot and as soon as we got in the car to start the trip home, a backseat brawl began. Without a moment's hesitation, my dad stopped the car and ordered us out! Now this was a whole new ballgame, being forced from the car many miles from home. Who knew how to get home from Seattle? I saw fear slide over the faces of Janet and Mary Ann as the Buick rolled slowly away and I knew this was a serious situation we were in.

"Stop," we all yelled.

We began to run after the car and relief came rushing in like the tide as we saw the car stop ahead. We opened the doors and hopped in without a word. Silence and obedience filled the backseat all the way home.

I'd like to say that was the last time we ever had a backseat brouhaha but that probably wasn't so.

Field Testing the
Blue Bomber

ON THE FARM, KIDS LEARN early to drive. I was about 10 years old when
I had my first behind the wheel experience in the old International truck.
When you are the third oldest child it seems your turn will never come,
when you will be the one steering the truck through the pasture while your
Dad pitches hay off the flat bed to the cows. Through default my opportunity came one day in 1945 and while the truck was put into low gear all
I had to do was keep my foot barely touching the gas pedal and steer about
the field in an already designated pattern. It was a piece of cake and no
one got hurt.

There were a few times however, when he looked like a surfer with a
pitchfork, trying to ride the big one. That's when I would hear him pound
on the cab, "My God", he'd yell, "Are you trying to kill me?"

With age came a little more responsibility and I was taught how to find
1st gear, put it in and keep slowly rolling around the field. Now, my dad
was a cowboy and had spent years riding bucking broncos so he was usually pretty good at riding the bucking International flatbed which could be
seen lurching and bucking around the field as I tried to master the manual
transmission where you shift and not the engine.

Working the hands and feet together on that big old squawking clutch and the squirrelly gear shift was no easy task.

As my sisters and I grew older and driving became our passion, we felt we had outgrown the old International and looked for a sportier ride. Janet, my oldest sister, and Mary Ann the next oldest were far more daring than I and tried driving the tractor a few times, usually with disastrous results, but I never tried that. Too big and scary for me.

As luck would have it, we had a neighbor down the road about a mile who would often come to visit our family. Sometimes he would come walking down the road, his sparsely covered head down, hands shoved inside the top of his bib overalls, looking for agates in the gravel between our house and his on McLean Road.

He went to Carl's Coffee Shop in LaConner every morning for coffee and conversation and to our house or other neighbors in the evenings. The rest of his day was consumed taking care of his low functioning Downs Syndrome brother who had become his total re-sponsibility when both of his elderly parents had died.. Robin was not a great conversationalist but

he was congenial and my parents didn't seem to mind that he was there all the time. Sometimes he would just sit on the porch, often he helped weed the garden but mostly he just watched the four of us kids play, some-times joining in a game of "Kick the Can" or "Tag".

On the evenings when he would come gliding into the barnyard be-hind the wheel of the "Blue Bomber", excitement ran high for that meant there would be a driving lesson. Had there been High School Driver Ed classes at that time, Robin would have been the perfect instructor for he was a man who had learned patience with a capital P in his daily life with his brother. He never screamed or shouted at you nor panicked like parents tend to do.

The "Blue Bomber" was a powder blue Plymouth Sedan, vintage late 30's, with suicide doors. It was as big as a great blue whale and seemed to slither along on its belly with running boards barely off the ground.

My sisters and I would run to the car, scrambling to be the first to reach driver position, the losers taking a spot in the back seat and Robin riding shotgun and helping maneuver the gnarly gear shift into all the appropriate positions. Usually we headed out behind the barn into a 40 acre pasture where there was little danger of hitting anything except maybe a fence post or a cow. Riding in the back seat was almost as much fun as being behind the wheel for you could pretend you were in a gangster movie outrunning the bad guys.

If the car was moving slowly you could open your suicide door, squat down on the running board, stick your Tommy gun through the open window and shoot at the ones chasing you.. It was great fun and a game we never tired of. . You could also open your back door, wrap an arm around the center post and ride standing on the running board, another gangster position. Miraculously we were never hurt and things that happened in the back 40 stayed in the back 40. Robin was no stool pigeon!

We all three mastered shifting, forward AND reverse, without any bucking, learned when to let out the clutch and when to press on the gas, making the transition from 1st to 3rd gear smooth as butter, learned to steer a straight line, learned how to start and stop with out any hiccups, learned all the appropriate hand signals and how to do a perfect figure eight without hitting a single cow.

When we each reached that magic age of 16, we were so ready for the DMV we could have taught them a few things. We all received our license on the first try, got the license and were on the road. Thanks to Robin.

My Sport

I THANK GOD, THE PRESIDENT, the senators and the House of Representatives for not enacting TITLE 9 while I was still in school for that would have made my life more miserable than it was on GYM day. Some politician or women's libber thought it would be more "even steven" if little girls could play sports like all the little boys and they changed the world.

Today teams of girls are running bases, scoring goals on soccer fields, slapping that ball over the net and bringing home championship trophies just like the boys. I admire this new breed of girl; their ability and fierce competitiveness.

I have three granddaughters who all have athletic ability: Arielle had ice skates attached to her feet almost as soon as she could walk and became a lovely figure skater. Sara was a gymnastic artist who became the flyer in the cheer leading squad all through her high school years. And Emma has amazed us all with her ability and determination on the track where she sets personal goals and breaks records at The Ohio State University. None of them have my non-athletic genes. For this I am thankful.

I would have failed miserably if this sporting scene had been part of my formative years for I had no athletic ability or inclination. When they were handing out sports I thought they said warts and said," Skip me."

Actually, my life was a happy one, each day filled with gleeful moments until it came to GYM period. When we were forced onto the baseball diamond I struck out every time: no eye/hand coordination. During my time in the outfield, I was silently praying the ball would not come in my direction. It's hard to catch a ball when your hands are clasped together in prayer! I wouldn't have recognized home plate if it tapped me on the shoulder. The only home plate I knew was heaped with meat and potatoes.

Coordination also failed me on the basketball court; couldn't hit the hoop if I was standing on a step ladder, and all that running back and forth, end to end. Exhausting!

Analyzing the sport situation, I think I was afraid of the ball hitting me in the face. When spring arrived and we adjourned to the tennis court, I had some minor success: the ball was small and the racquet was a weapon.

However, when I discovered a sport where there was no ball involved, I jumped in with both feet and learned to roller skate. It was challenging to find a skating venue when living on a farm: no sidewalks or paved streets so we mostly skated in barns or cement aprons outside the barn which required sweeping aside hay and scraping up cow pies first.

In the beginning I had expandable metal skates with metal wheels which would fit your shoes as you grew so they lasted for many years. As long as you didn't lose the skate key you were in business. The worst that could happen was skinned knees. Band aids and mercurochrome the simple solution.

As I grew older I graduated to the Burlington Roller Rink where you could find me every Friday night. I'm afraid I forgot to thank my parents for driving me there each week. At home in bed after hours of skating, my legs would still be buzzing as I awaited sleep.

One year for my birthday I received my very own shoe skates in a shiny metal suitcase. No more renting skates at the rink. It was undoubtedly the best gift I have ever received and I wore them, always spotlessly polished, for many years. I became a pretty respectable skater and loved gliding around the rink in time to the beautiful dance music from the Wurlitzer.

I seldom fell, skated frontward and backwards and could do the Skaters Waltz with a partner. I never felt the need to compete in any skating groups, never had any desire to become a Roller Derby Queen, I just don't have that mean or aggressive streak in me.

Roller skating was my life for a few years and sometimes I wish I could still do it but I know better, for my balance is not so good and the bones are brittle. Every time I hear an organ playing the Skaters Waltz I silently dream of being out there on those smooth oak boards.

Dasterdly Crimes in Nursery Rhymes

∽⌒

I GREW UP BEING SCARED of my own shadow and everything else on the farm. I always wondered what had caused that and now at last, I think I have found the one responsible; MOTHER GOOSE.

Most nights, as we lay snuggled down in our beds, awaiting sleep, one of our parents would read from the Big Mother Goose book of Nursery Rhymes as part of the bedtime ritual. What were they thinking? Most of those legendary rhymes are frightening; full of mischief, murder and mayhem. Perhaps I took them too literally but they filled my head with terrible thoughts that were not conducive to sleep.

I thought we were to be kind to all Gods creatures but the author of Nursery Rhymes seemed to have a vendetta against birds as in;

Away birds away
Take a Little, Leave a little
And do not come again
For if you do
I will shoot you through
And that will be the end of you.

Then there was that one about;
"Who killed Cock Robin
I said the sparrow
With my bow and arrow. "

And it wasn't just birds, there were a lot of rhymes where cats were the victims. Remember

"Ding, Dong Bell
Pussy in the Well?

That's the one where "Little Johnny Stout tries to drown poor Pussy. Nothing funny about that. Johnny should have had some psychiatric evaluation for that is often an indication he could become a psychotic killer later in life. These kinds of stories troubled me.

I worried about the children of the "Old Woman who lived in a shoe "
She had so many children
She didn't know what to do
She gave them some broth without
Any bread

She whipped them all soundly and put them to bed. That's child abuse.

They didn't deserve a whipping. What had they done wrong? Nothing. I think this situation is a strong case for Planned Parenthood and maybe she should have applied for food stamps so she could feed her children. I couldn't sleep a wink after this one.

And what about "Old Mother Hubbard?" She was the one who had no food in her cupboard. Not even a bone for her dog. I guess times were tough then for a lot of people and for dogs.

"She went to the baker
To buy him some bread
And when she came back
The dog was dead"

This one made me cry. How could I go to sleep? "No more, no more!"

Oh but there is more. More violence, more cruelty, more abuse.

How about

"Little Polly Flinders who sat among the cinders
Warming her pretty little toes
Her mother came and caught her
Whipped her little daughter
For spoiling her nice new clothes."

Child abuse! It sort of sounded like something that could have happened to me. I was forever getting into places I didn't belong and being caught. A whipping sounded worse than a spanking, with which I was quite familiar. Another sleepless night.

The rhymes were full of all kinds of abuse; child abuse, animal abuse and even elder abuse, as in Goosey Gander. Remember that one? It starts out nice enough describing Goosey wandering aimlessly about and then in the second verse he gets violent when he

"Meets an old man
Who wouldn't say his prayers
So he grabbed him by his left leg
And threw him down the stairs."

Now isn't that a sad thing to think about when you're trying to fall asleep? I shed a few tears as I pictured an old Grandpa lying at the foot of the stairs in a pile of broken bones and maybe a cut on his head with blood pouring out onto the floor. Will he live?

Do you recall the rhyme about the Old Woman and the Peddler? I thought of my Grandma, Mary Jane, when I heard this one.

"There came a peddler whose name was Stout
He cut her petticoats all round about
He cut her petticoats up to her knees
Which made the old woman shiver and freeze"

Was Stout arrested and charged with assault? Probably not.

Is it any wonder I was afraid of everything after listening to Mother Goose night after night? Sometimes Mother Goose was put aside and Grimm's Fairy Tales took over but that was no better. In the story of Little Red Riding Hood where she finds the big bad wolf in Grandma's bed, wearing her nightgown and ruffled night cap, did you ever wonder what had happened to Grandma? I did. I worried all night that she was locked in a closet somewhere where no one would find her, she might run out of air and die.

Okay, I guess Mother Goose and Mr. Grimm are both responsible for the way I was a fraidy cat.

Made in the USA
Columbia, SC
07 June 2017